J. Wickham Legg

The Processional of the Nuns of Chester

J. Wickham Legg

The Processional of the Nuns of Chester

ISBN/EAN: 9783337140793

Printed in Europe, USA, Canada, Australia, Japan

Cover: Foto ©Lupo / pixelio.de

More available books at **www.hansebooks.com**

HENRY BRADSHAW SOCIETY

Founded in the Year of Our Lord 1890

for the editing of Rare Liturgical Texts.

VOL. XVIII.

ISSUED TO MEMBERS FOR THE YEAR 1899,

AND

PRINTED FOR THE SOCIETY

BY

HARRISON AND SONS, ST. MARTIN'S LANE,

PRINTERS IN ORDINARY TO HER MAJESTY.

THE

PROCESSIONAL

OF THE

NUNS OF CHESTER

EDITED FROM A MANUSCRIPT IN THE POSSESSION OF THE EARL OF ELLESMERE AT BRIDGEWATER HOUSE

BY

J. WICKHAM LEGG,

Fellow of the Royal College of Physicians and of the Society of Antiquaries of London.

London.

1899

INTRODUCTION.

THE manuscript now edited was first brought to my notice by Mr. Barclay Squire, F.S.A., of the British Museum, in the late autumn of 1898. It is one of the collection of manuscripts at Bridgewater House belonging to the Earl of Ellesmere. By his permission the manuscript is now edited for the Henry Bradshaw Society, and I have to thank him for his kindness and patience in allowing the manuscript to be deposited at the British Museum during the long time necessary for its transcription and printing.

This manuscript is connected with the nuns of Chester by the writing at the end of the book: *This booke longeth to Dame Margery Byrkenhed of Chestre.* The directions on Palm Sunday and Shere Thursday make it plain that the book was written for a convent of women, and there was a monastery of Benedictine nuns at Chester under the invocation of St. Mary. The patron of the church for which this book was written seems to be our Lady, as her altar is the first named in the ceremonies of Shere Thursday, and there is an abundance of anthems and hymns in her honour, somewhat beyond what is usual. St. Benedict also is marked by a procession on his day in March and in July, and by other memorials. The requirements of these phænomena would be satisfied by ascribing this book to the Benedictine Nunnery of St. Mary at Chester.

From the liturgical point of view the book is a processional, to which the rubrics testify with their frequent use of the word "procession"; and, further, a short examination will satisfy an inquirer that the earlier part of the book is in direct affinity with the processionals of Sarum and York. Towards the end a number of private prayers appear; and quite at the end, the hand, as well as the tongue, change into the ordinary and vernacular.

A noteworthy feature of this manuscript is the presence of rubrics in English. But the English is not often more than the name of the day, except in the services for Candlemas, Palm Sunday, and Shere Thursday.

The books of the nuns of Syon sometimes show English rubrics. At Magdalene College, Cambridge, there is a Syon psalter, prefixed to which is an Ordinal with English rubrics. Its press mark is G. 14. 11. At St. John's College, Cambridge (press mark: Theo. C. S. while A. 6. 11. is erased) and at St. John's College, Oxford (MS. No. 167.) there are processionals, which once belonged to the same order, with rubrics in English. But in these last, like the processional of the Chester nuns, the English rubrics are for the most part limited to the name of the day, while full rubrics are found in the manuscript Psalter. The nuns of this Brigittine Order seem to have had a liking for vernacular rubrics. In the *Breviarium Sororum ac Sanctimonialium Sacri Ordinis Divae Brigittae* (Atrebati, Rob. Maudhuy, 1610, 4°) the *Rubriques ou Directoire de ce Breviaire* of the first three leaves will be found in French, and at the end of the book occur offices with the rubrics in French. The prayers themselves are in Latin.

So also there is an Italian manuscript of Brigittine use in the Bodleian Library at Oxford in which the greater part of the book is in Latin, but here and there Italian sentences come out. (MS. Canonici Liturg. 49 [19249] ff. 12*b*. and 325*b*.) I have not knowledge enough of processionals to say if the use of vernacular rubrics be common in these books, apart from those of nuns; but I may mention that in the Ambrosian rite, the early printed processionals have vernacular rubrics. One (Mediolani, Leonard Pachel, 1501, 8°) and another (Mediolani, Vincentius Giardonius, 1567, 8°), containing the processions for Rogation days, which are kept in the first week after the Ascension in this church, have the rubrics in Italian throughout. But in a third (Mediolani, Amb. Sirturi, 1657, 8°), ninety years after the latter, the rubrics are throughout in Latin. Of much later books with the rubrics in the vernacular, such as the *Rituel d'Alet*, it is not necessary here to speak.

It cannot be said that this book gives us great insight into the rites of the monastery at Chester. There is an octave for Candlemas; but not for the Conception, or the Visitation of our [illegible]e of which at the end of the other festivals may [illegible]nt introduction. There seems nothing very noteworthy [illegible] the ceremonies of Candlemas. The same may be said of Palm Sunday, if we except the "City of Jerusalem," which was perhaps some place higher than the rest from which the anthems were sung; but this is guess work. There is no evidence given of the carrying of the Blessed Sacrament in the procession on this day, a custom once common all over England.

The old rule of a maundy on Saturdays seems to have survived at all events for the Saturdays after Easter. The little that is known of the history of the house, with the documents of the suppression in the time of Henry VIII. may be found in Ormerod.[1]

In the British Museum (MS. Harl. 2073, fo. 87) there is a "ground plot of St. Maryes Abby or the Nunes" made in the reign of Queen Elizabeth. Unfortunately the plan is of little use to one endeavouring to recover the outlines of the mediæval house, as the alterations made after the suppression are seen to be very considerable. Of the building at this moment nothing seems to remain. "Of the priory of the Benedictine nuns at Chester scarcely any traces now exist, except the name of the Nuns Gardens, preserved in the site of that monastery near the castle: some of the buildings appear to have been standing in the year 1729 when Buck's View of Chester Castle was published."[2]

[1] George Ormerod, *History of the County Palatine and City of Chester*, London, 1882, vol. i. p. 346. See also Thomas Tanner, *Notitia Monastica*, Ed. James Nasmith, Cambridge, 1787. Cheshire, vii. 3.

[2] Daniel and Samuel Lysons, *Magna Britannia*, London, 1810, vol. ii. Part ii. p. 453. An engraving of the ground plot from Harl. 2073 is given in this volume.

Of Dame Margery Birkenhed I have been able to gain no precise information. It was a custom for ecclesiastics and religious persons to take the name of the place from which they came, of which we have familiar examples in the case of William of Wykeham and William of Waynflete. So that the Dame's family name may not have been Birkenhead. But in the family of Birkenhead of Huxley the name Margaret sometimes occurs, as Mr. Barclay Squire has pointed out to me in their pedigree.[1] Further than this it does not seem possible to go.

The manuscript has not been reproduced in full. For example, no attempt has been made to print any part of the music. This was examined by Mr. W. J. Birkbeck, F.S.A., and was found to show the ordinary characters of the music of the Sarum books; so that it was not thought worth while to reproduce all of it. Further, the whole of the anthems, responds, and collects has not been always printed. Whenever one of these could be discovered without much trouble in English books that have been made accessible of late years, such as the Sarum or York processional, missal, or breviary, or the Westminster missal, then the liturgical form has only been printed in part: the first and last words being given with a reference in the text to the book where it may be found. The anthems are for the most part well known. Exact verbal correspondence is not meant to be implied; but, in choosing the book to which reference has been given, that has been taken as a rule which gives a form nearest akin to that in the manuscript. Generally speaking, the forms in the manuscript are more like those in the Sarum than in the York books. Chester it may be remembered was in the diocese of Lichfield, and thus part of the province of Canterbury, until the changes in Henry VIII.'s time. Where the form is short, even if it be found in the books mentioned, it has been sometimes given in full: and in this case the reference has not been always given in the text, but in the notes, where references have been given to the forms where such have been traced;

[1] See Harl. MS. 1535, fo. 78*b*.

references to those in an English book have been given in every possible case, and it may be added that in most cases where the forms have been found in an English book it has not been thought worth while to follow their history further into books that come from across the sea.

Of the remaining longer forms, printed in full, most of them can be found in other liturgical books. References to these are also given in the notes at the end of this volume.

The musical notation is limited to the anthems and hymns; the collects, verses, and the cues to the anthems are not noted. Almost all the anthems, if not all, up to p. 19 of the following edition, have musical notation, but after this the notes cease until p. 25, when some of the anthems have notes over them. In order to give an idea of the musical notation, and of the writing of the book, three pages in collotype reproducing the carol *Qui creavit celum* (p. 18.) are added to this edition.

The words written in black have been printed in Roman type, while those written in red are printed in italics. Also it may be well to point out that, in printing, two methods of dealing with the contractions have been adopted, according as the words are English or Latin. The Latin has been expanded without any indication of the letters supplied; but when the English words have been expanded the letters supplied are given in a fount different from that of the rest of the word: for example, when the word or sentence generally is in italics, the letters supplied in the expansion are given in roman; when the word is in roman, the letters supplied are in italics.

The mediæval spelling has been followed in all cases and no attempt made to reduce the Latin to the ordinary standard. So that in some cases where the spelling or reading may appear strange, it is the manuscript itself that is at fault. When it has been wished to call attention to the reading as being that of the manuscript itself, an obelus has been inserted after the word.

Some of the readings in the metrical hymns are very unlike what is met with in other texts, and can hardly be construed;

for example, the variations in *Tellus ac ethera* (p. 10) are so many that it was thought better not to use the obelus; but the printed text, whatever its curiosities may be, has been very carefully compared with the manuscript, and follows it as closely as may be.

It may be held that these variations indicate a careless scribe, and it is some evidence that the book has not been much in use, that no marks suggesting alterations appear in the margin. A book in the British Museum (Add. MS. 30,514) formerly in use by the nuns of Syon has been carefully gone through by a corrector, and faults indicated by a cross in the margin; which have been accordingly corrected.

The manuscript is written in red and black, with decorated initials; while the rubrics are in red, the body of the work is in black. Mr. Warner of the British Museum assigns the writing of the greater part of the book to a date near 1425, but not much before that year, while the writing of the end of the book is much later than this. The writing of the fly-leaves at the beginning and end of the book he assigns to the end of the fifteenth century.

The leaves of the book are vellum and 85 in number, though the number of the leaves has not yet been marked on them. They measure on their outer edge 140 mm. by 197 mm., that is, about 6½ inches broad by 8 inches high. The first six leaves are somewhat coarser in texture than the others and they are blank, except that on the two middle leaves there is an anthem or two written and noted. With Mr. Warner's assistance I have made out the structure of the manuscript to be as shown by the following diagram:

$$a^6\ A^8\ B^9\ C^8\ D—G^9\ H^8\ I^8\ K^2\ L^1.$$

In the gatherings with 9 leaves there is one inserted leaf; but it is not constant in the place at which it is inserted.

When the music takes up a whole page, there are seven lines; without music twenty-one lines.

The book has been recently bound in dark morocco. The crest of the family of Egerton is stamped in gold on both covers, surmounted by an earl's coronet. The book is lettered on the back: *Missal of Dame Margery Birkenhead.* Lower down is: *MS.*

The private prayers and hymns written in an ordinary hand at the end of the book have been transcribed by Mr. Barclay Squire, and I am indebted to him for the permission to print them from his copy, and for much help kindly given me in this undertaking. I would also express my thanks to Mr. G. F. Warner, for help in matters connected with palæography; to Mr. Henry Jenner, F.S.A., and Mr. Robert G. C. Proctor, for help in other matters. And above all, to my colleagues in the Society, Mr. Dewick and Mr. H. A. Wilson, whose kindness and consideration for me know no bounds.

For the General Index I am indebted to my son.

SYMBOLS.

The following symbols have been used in this edition :

S : *Processionale ad usum insignis ac praeclarae Ecclesiae Sarum* Leeds, 1882, ed. W. G. Henderson.

S. B : *Breviarium ad usum insignis Ecclesiae Sarum*, Cantabrig. 1879-1886. in three fasciculi, ed. Procter and Wordsworth.

S. M : *Missale ad usum insignis et praeclarae Ecclesiae Sarum*, Burntisland, 1861-1883, ed. F. H. Dickinson.

W : *Missale ad usum Ecclesiae Westmonasteriensis*, Henry Bradshaw Society, 1891-97, in three fasciculi.

Y : *Manuale et Processionale ad usum insignis Ecclesiae Eboracensis*, Surtees Society, 1875, ed. W. G. Henderson.

Y. B : *Breviarium ad usum insignis Ecclesiae Eboracensis*, Surtees Society, 1880-1883, in two volumes, ed. S. W. Lawley.

On Sondays in the Aduent. say thys antem.[1]

MIssus est angelus gabriel . . . uerbum tuum alleluya. [S. 6.]

The antems of owre Lady say on Sonday. one & a nother a nother.

a' De te uirgo.
an. Quo modo fiet istud.
an. Rorate celi desuper.

Procession of Seynct nicholas. Responsory.

QUi cum audissent sancti nicholai . . . clemenciam.
℣. Clara quippe . . . famulum. Saluatoris. [S. B. iii. 31.]

In the concepcion of owre lady this .℟.

UErbum patris mundo fulsit
virginis per vterum
cuius mentem non grauauit
onus premens scelerum.
Ut super vellus pluuia.
Sic descendit in maria.
℣. Solem iusticie concludunt claustra marie. Ut super.

[1] *On two out of the six flyleaves at the beginning of the book is written with musical notes:*

Et nunc sequimur in toto corde et timemus te et querimus faciem tuam domine nec confundas nos sed fac nobis iuxta mansuetudinem tuam et secundum multitudinem misericordie tue.

Amo christum in cuius talamum introiui cuius mater virgo est cuius pater femina† nescit cuius michi organum† modulatis vocibus cantant quem cum amauero casta sum cum tetigero munda sum cum accepero virgo sum.

On cristenmas day procession .℟.

DEscendit de celis . . . fabrice mundi.

℣. Tanquam sponsus . . . thalamo suo. Et exiuit. Gloria patri et filio et spiritui sancto. Et exiuit. [S. 12.]

If it falle on Sonday. ye shal say this .a'.

HOdie christus natus . . . excelsis deo alleluya. [S. 13.]

℣. Puer natus est nobis.

On Sonday afftur yole day thys procession. ℟

IN principio erat verbum . . . factum est nichil. [Iohan. i. 1—3.]

℣. Quod factum est in ipso uita erat et vita erat lux hominum. Omnia.

a'. Hodie christus natus est hodie.

℣. Puer natus.

Byfore at the euynsong of seynt Iohn say this .℟.

HIc est discipulus qui testimonium perhibet de hiis. Et scripsit hec et scimus quia uerum est testimonium eius.

℣. Fluenta euangelii de ipso sacro dominici pectoris fonte potauit. Et scripsit hec

[1]*To seynt thomas*[1] *procession*. ℟.

Ex summa rerum . . . populo leticia.

℣. Concurrit turba . . . beneficiorum. Sed cum. ℣.† [S. B. i. cclii.]

On newyers da thys procession. ℟.

UErbum caro factum . . . ueritatis.

℣. In principio . . . uerbum. Cuius. gloriam.[2] [S. 21.]

On twelfe day. procession. ℟.

IN columbe specie . . . audite.

℣. Celi aperti . . . audita est. c est. [Y. 143.]

If itt fall on a Sonday ze shall say this A'.

HOdie celesti sponso . . . conuiue alleluya. [S. B. i. cccxxx.]

℣. Et intrantes domum.

1—1 *struck through with black line, probably in Henry VIII.'s time.*

2 *In margin is written*; a' [a word illegible] virgo hodie ℣. verbum. The procession the Sonday next after new yeres day. Verbum.

REx magnus natus est in israhel et uenerunt reges terre adorare eum. Et optulerunt ei munera aurum thus et mirram.

℣. Et intrantes domum inuenerunt puerum cum maria matre eius et procidentes adorauerunt eum. Et optulerunt.

a'. Hodie celesti.

℣. Et intrantes.

*On Sondaies betwene the vtas of the epiphanie and septuagesime processio. Ant*em.

O maria iesse virga celi regina maris stella plenitudo temporis ecce iam venit iam olim promissum florem protulisti ergo precamur o domina vt qui te meruimus confiteri christi matrem senciamus o pia ut singulari merito hunc nobis tu facias placabilem et dies istos tue sancte uirginitatis partu nobis ipse propter te o benignissima disponas quo temporalis solennitas nos ad eternam enutriat leticiam alleluya.

a'. Uirgo hodie fidelis. ℣.†

On candlemas day when candles *by*n *halowed the prest shalbegyn this .ps.*

LUmen ad reuelationem gencium et gloriam plebis tue israhel.

ps. Nunc dimittis seruum tuum domine secundum verbum tuum in pace.

ps. Lumen.

Quia uiderunt oculi mei salutare tuum.

Lumen.

Quod parasti ante faciem omnium populorum.

Lumen.

Aue gratia plena dei genitrix uirgo ex te enim ortus est sol iusticie.

here shalbe the goyng owte of the stallis to the churche dor

illuminans qui in tenebris sunt . . . nobis et resurrectionem. [S. 143.]

Oute at yͤ churche dore with this .a'.

ADorna thalamum . . . saluatorem mundi. [S. 143.]

At the frater doore begyn thys antym.

REsponsum accepit . . . . tuum in pace. [S. 144.]

At the parlowr dore begyn thys antym.

HOdie beata virgo . . . accepit eum [S. 144.]

CUm inducerent puerum iesum tuum in pace.
[S. B. iii. 41.]
℣. Symeon iustus.

On sonday withine the vtas of candlemas.

NUnc dimittis . . . salutare tuum.
℣. Quod parasti . . . reuelationem gencium. Quia. [S. 143.]

HOdie maria uirgo puerum offert in templo quem symeon senex accepit in brachiis et anna vidua christum agnouit aduenisse in terris.
℣. [1]simion iustus.[1]

This procession shalbe saide on Sonday & so forth fro septuagesime to lenton.

ECce carissimi . . . regna celorum.
℣. Ecce mater . . . uenite ad me. Ut. ℣.† [S. 24.]

The fyrst sonday of lenton and so to the passion Sonday this seruis to procession.

CHriste pater. misericordiarum qui tempus acceptabile reis indulges reminiscere miserationum tuarum et quos hucusque tolleras ad penitenciam compunge peccauimus domine in omnem iusticiam tuam et iniquitates nostre abstulerunt nos et tu iratus es et auertisti faciem tuam et possiderunt nos domine absque te et respice tu pater noster es et nos lutum ne irascaris nobis neque multitudinem viscerum tuorum super nos contineas vltra. Sed parce placare attende et fac nobis iuxta multitudinem benignitatis tue ut in die bona quam tu fecisti o fons dauid patens in ablucione menstruate ne confundantur† in nobis sed letemur in te.

Say iche Sonday one of these .a'. of oure laidy.
a'. Anima mea.
a'. Descendi in ortum.
a'. Beata dei genitrix.
℣. Post partum uirgo.

On Seynct benet day this procession

O felix benedicte iam de tua gloria secure nostris miseriis curam impende. Per christum excusa mala que fecimus et obtine bona que poscimus.

[1]—[1] *added in later hand.*

℣. Ut cruciatus infernorum possimus cuadere et de dei conspectu tecum gaudere. Per.

℣. [1]Os iusti[1]

On passion Sonday y^is. ℟.

MUltiplicati sunt . . . deus meus.

℣. Nequando dicat . . . eum. Exurge. [S. B. i. dccxix.]

℣. Dederunt in escam meam fel.

a'. Descendi in ortum meum.

On palme Sonday when palmes is[2] *blessed. the prest shalbegyn.* *.a'*. Pueri. *and the chauntres shal take* hebreorum. *and soo forth synge this.*

PUeri hebreorum tollentes . . excelsis. [S. 47.]

the chauntres shall begyn this antym

PUeri hebreorum uestimenta . . nomine domini [S. 47.]

here shalbe the first entre oute of the qwere w^t thys. a'.

ANte sex dies . . . uoce magna dicentes osanna in excelsis. [S. 49.]

fro the churche doore to ierusalem ye shal say thys antym.

CUm appropinquaret dominus . . . miserere nobis fili dauid. [S. 48.]

Here the priores and other .ij. ladies shall take the prestes & goo in to the cyte of ierusalem and there thay shal synge this antym.

EN rex uenit . . . lectio prophetica. [S. 50.]

Here the ladies that ben with oute shall synge this .a'. when they come to ierusalem. thai shal knele downe & also at yche .a'. y^t thay synge.

SAlue quem ihesum testatur . . . uerba salutis. [S. 50.]

The Priores and hire felous this antym.

HIc est qui de edom . . . altis curribus. [S. 51.]

Tho that ben withoute commande toward the priores and she to theym thys antym.

SAlue lux mundi rex regum . hic et in euum. [S. 51.]

[1]—[1] *added in later hand.*
[2] *interlined in blue letters.*

The priores and hiere felows comande toward those y^t ben thereoute w^t this antym.

HIc est ille qui ut agnus . . . quandam beati vates prompserunt prophetice. [S. 51.]

Tho there out comyng to gedre say this .a'.

SAlue nostra salus . . . iura subisti [S. 51.]

Then shall all go to the hye crosse in *the churcheyarde syngynge y^is antym and the prestes before theym.*

CUm audisset populus . . . redimere nos. [S. 49.]

When thay comen to the crosse on the northe halff a decon shall reede a gospell. Cum appropinquaret. *when itt is redd the prest shall knele down thryse & synge.*

DIgnus es domine . . . et honorem.

OCcurrunt turbe . nubila osanna. [S. 51.]

W^t thys antym and y^is Responsory y^ai shal goo to the churche dore & w^t this verse

COllegerunt . . . gentem.

℣. Unus autem . . . dicentes. Ne forte [S. 52.]

Here the .ij. chauntres shal take .ij. ladies into *the churche & synge these ℣.*

GLoria laus . . ecce tibi. [S. 52.]

Here thay shall goo in to the crosse w^t thys. antym.

INgrediente domino . . . in excelsis.

℣. Cunque audissent populus . . . obuiam ei. Cum [S. 53.]

When thai comyn before the cros. the prest shal go knele downe thries & syng

AUe rex noster . . . osanna in excelsis. Aue rex. [S. 53.]

In to the Qwhere w^t this .a'.

CIrcumdederunt me . . vindica me.

℣. Quoniam tribulacio . . . adiuuet. Sed. [S. 43.]

℣. Dederunt in escam meam fel.

On sherthursday at the washyng of the auters y^s ℟.

IN monte oliueti . . . uoluntas tua.

℣. Uerumptamen . . . sicut tu uis. Fiat. [S. 60.]

℟. TRistis est anima mea . . . pro vobis.

℣. Ecce appropinquabit . . . peccatorum [S. 61.]

antym.

O iuda qui dereliquisti . . . habebas.

℣. Os tuum habundauit . . . dolos. Et. [S. 63.]

℣. Christus factus est pro nobis obediens.

Oracio.

REspice quesumus domine . tormentum. Per. [S. B. i. dcclxxii.]

Goo to seynt mary auter wt thys antym of the assumpcion.

AScendit christus . . . existit. [S. 154.]

℣. Exaltata est† sancta dei genitrix.

Oracio

UEneranda nobis . . . genuit incarnatum. Qui tecum viuit et regnat. [S. 154.]

Of Seynt Iohn the euangelist say this antym.

IOhannes apostolus & euangelista virgo est electus a domino atque inter ceteros magis dilectus.

℣. Ualde honorandus est beatus iohannes.

Oracio.

ECclesiam tuam . . . iohannis euangeliste sempiterna. Per. [S. 17.]

Of Seynct Iames yis antym.

O beate iacobe qui subuenis periclitantibus ad te clamantibus tam in mari quam in terra succurre nobis & in periculo mortis.

℣. Ora pro nobis beate iacobe.

oracio

ESto domine . . . secura deseruiat. Per. [S. B. iii. 533.]

Of Seynt nicholas this .a'.

BEatus nicholaus adhuc puerulus multo ieiunio macerabat corpus.

℣. Ora pro nobis beate nicholae.

oracio

DEus qui beatum nicholaum pium pontificem tuum . . . . incendiis liberemur. Per. [S. B. iii. 25.]

[Here a rubric relating to St. Edmund should have been written.]

NOn est inuentus similis illi qui conseruaret legem excelsi.

℣. Ora pro nobis beate Edmunde

Oracio

DEus qui largiflue bonitatis . . . patrociniis protegamur aduersis. Per. [S. B. iii. 1053.]

Of Seynt Benet this .a'.

DEi repletus gratia
benedictus ab infancia
contempsit huius infima

mundi sequens celestia.

℣. Os iusti meditabitur sapiencia.

Oracio

INtercessio nos domine quesumus beati benedicti abbatis . . . patrocinio assequamur. Per. [S. B. iii. 467.]

Of Seynct Margarete thys antym.

ERat autem margareta annorum quindecim cum ab impio olibrio tradebatur in carcere.

℣ Ora pro nobis beata margareta.

Oracio

DEus qui beatam margaretam . . . peruenire mereamur. Per. [S. B. iii. 501.]

Of Seynt Thomas this antym.

EGo sum pastor bonus qui pasco oues meas & pro ouibus meis pono animam meam.

℣. Ora pro nobis beate thoma.

oracio

DEus pro cuius ecclesia gloriosus pontifex . . . salutarem consequantur effectum. Per. [S. B. i. ccxlvi.]

Of Seynct katerine this .a'.

IN bello victus constantinoque fugatus
alexandrinam uenit maxencius urbem.

℣. Ora pro nobis beata katerina.

Oracio

DEus qui dedisti legem moysi . . . valeamus peruenire. Per. [S. B. iii. 1103.]

Of Seynt Anne thys antym.

ANna deo vigilauit eo quod lucis alumpna
hanc genuit que virgo fuit vicequet columpna.

℣. Interueni pro nobis beata mater anna.

Oracio.

PResta domine fidelibus tuis beate matris anne digna veneracione natalicia peruenire ⁄ de cuius sacra carne vnigeniti tui genitrix ad natiuitatis humane processit dies que mundo salua virginitate lucis eterne parturiuit auctorem. Per.

Of Seynct marie magdaleyn .y^is .a'.

MAgdalenam sua crimina confitentem christus dominus suscepit et emundatam in pace abire precepit.

℣. Dimissa sunt ei peccata multa.

Oracio

LArgire nobis clementissime . . . . impetret beatitudinem. Per. [Y. B. ii. 398.]

Of Seynt. Iohn the baptist.

ELizabeth zacharie magnum virum genuit iohannem baptistam percursorem domini.

℣. Fuit homo missus a deo.

Oracio

OMnipotens sempiterne deus da cordibus nostris illam tuarum rectitudinem semitarum quam beatus iohannes baptista in deserto vox clamantis edocuit. Per.

Of all halowes this antym shalbe saide.

GAudent in celis anime sanctorum qui christi uestigia sunt sequuti et quia pro eius amore sanguinem suum fuderunt ideo cum christo regnabunt ineternum.

℣. Orate pro nobis omnes sancti dei.

Oracio

COncede quesumus . . . patrocinia senciamus. Per eundem. [S. 63.]

a' Aue regina celorum.

At yͤ greate maundy afftur the washyng of the auters.

*At the first entre of the priores in to the chapiture to washe hiere Sistres feete on the Suppriores halfe thies antyms shall be songon that is to wete. antiph*ona.

Mandatum nouum.

a'. Si ego.

a'. Postquam surrexit.

a'. In diebus illis.

Antiphona

MAndatum nouum . . . dicit dominus. [S. 64.]

Ps. Beati immaculati in via qui ambulant in lege domini.

SI ego dominus . . . lauare pedes [S. 65.]

A'. POstquam surrexit . . . reliquit suis [S. 65.]

a' IN diebus illis . . . vnguento vngebat. [S. 65.]

Also at the secund entre of the Priores to washe the feete. This antym shall be songon on that other syde.

ACcepit maria libram vnguenti nardi pistici preciosi & vnxit pedes ihesu et capillis suis extersit stans retro vt peccatrix secus pedes domini eos lacrimis osculando rigauit.

*At the thred entre of the priores to weshe hiere hand*es *on the Suppriores halff this antym shall be songon.*

ANte diem . . . pedes discipulorum. [S. 65.]

At the .iiij.th entre of the priores to washe hire handeˢ on yᵗ oyer side yⁱˢ shalbe songone.

VEnit ad petrum . . . et caput. [S. 65.]

Here the priores shall cum in and sytt down in hiere chayre and that while the suppriores and other two of the aldist ladies shall ordeyn theim to wash the priores fete.

TEllus ac ethera iubilent
in cena magna principis
que prothoplausti pecora
vite purgauit fercula.
℣. Hac nocte factor omnium
potens ad ministerium
carnem suam cum sanguine
in escam transfert anime.
℣. Excelsus surgens dapibus
prebet formam mortalibus
humilitatis gracia
petri prebens vestigia.
℣. Pellet seruos obsequio
cum angelorum domino
ferendo limam lintheo
cernit ceno procumbere.
℣. Permitte symon ablui
acta figura mistica
dum sumus imo baiula
quod sanctus seruet cineri.
℣. Lauator thoris accubat
verbique faues aggerat
quos inter hostem deuota
nescis qui dolos ruminat.
℣. Trux lupe iuda pessime
ferago miti basia
das membra loris regia
que sorde tergunt secula.
℣. Noxi soluentur hodie
carnis a corde carcere
vngunt sacrati crismatis
spes inde crescat miseris.
℣. Victori mortis inclitam
pangamus laude gloriam
cum patre sancto spiritu
quos nos redemit habitu. Amen.

At the secund comynge of the suppriores to washe the Priores feete thys antym shall be songon.

COngregauit nos christus ad glorificandum se ipsum reple domine animas nostras sancto spiritu.

a'. Congregauit nos in vnum christi amor timeamus & amemus christum regem ubi caritas et amor ibi deus.

At the thrid comyng of the suppriores to washe the priores handes syng this.

DOmum istam . . . muros eius. [S. B. i. mcccclviii.]
Ps. Fundamenta eius . . . tabernacula iacob. [Ps. 86. v. 1.]
a' Domum istam.
Ps. Gloriosa dicta sunt de te ciuitas dei. [Ps. 86. v. 2.]
a'. Domum.
And at that other comyng thay shal syng. Ecce quam bonum. *and then thay shal rede a lesson. and then goo to the ffraytur.*

The first seturday afft^r paske this .a'. as on shere thurseday.
Mandatum nouum. [S. 64.]
A'. IN hoc cognoscent omnes quia mei estis discipuli si dilectionem habueritis adinuicem.

DIligamus nos in† inuicem quia caritas ex deo est et qui diligit fratrem suum ex deo natus est & videt deum ubi est caritas et dilectio ibi sanctorum est congregacio ibi nec ira nec indignacio sed firma caritas imperpetuum christus descendit mundum redimere vt liberaret a morte homines exemplum prebuit suis discipulis vt sibi inuicem pedes abluerent.

IHesum qui crucifixus est queritis alleluya non est hic surrexit enim sicut dixit vobis alleluia.

ARdens est cor meum desidero uidere dominum meum quero et non inuenio ubi posuerunt eum alleluya.
At the secund entre of the minist^e s† this .añ.
Ihesum qui crucifixus
ye shal not say. Congregauit. *but* Domum istam. Ecce quam bonum.

The secunde Seturday aftur paske day & so to the ascension of owre lorde this maundith
Mandatum nouum.
In hoc cognoscent.
Diligamus nos.
At ye secund comyng in. these iiij. A'.

MAria stabat . . . caput ihesu alleluia [S. B. i. dcccxl.]

DUm flerem ad monumentum vidi dominum meum alleluya.

VEnit maria nuncians discipulis quia vidi dominum alleluia.

TUlerunt dominum eum tollam alleluia alleluia. [S. B. i. dcccxli.]

The first Seturday aftur the Ascension day this maundi.
Mandatum nouum.

In *hoc*[1] cognoscent.

Diligamus.

ye shalnot say. Congregauit. *but in stede of it. say this .a'.*

MAria ergo vnxit pedes ihesu et extersit capillis suis et domus impleta est ex odore unguenti.

℣ Dimissa sunt ei peccata multa quoniam dilexit multum.

a'. Maria ergo.

a'. Domum istam.

Ps. Ecce quam bonum.

yche sonday to the ascension yis shalbe procession .℟

SEdit angelus . . . cum eo surrexit alleluya.

℣. Crucifixum . . . adorate. [S. B. i. dccсxxix.]

℟. Nolite.

CHristus resurgens . . . viuit deo alleluya alleluia. [S. B. dcccvii.]

℣. Dicite in nacionibus.

On the holy rode day. at euensonge.

PEr tuam crucem . . . resurgendo reparasti.

℣. Miserere nobis iesu . . . pro nobis.

Et vitam. Gloria patri . . . sancto.

Et. [S. 156.]

In the Ascension of or lord this procession.

VIri galilei . . . ita ueniet alleluia alleluya alleluia. [S. 123.]

℣. Cunque intuerentur . . . dixerunt.

Quemadmodum. [S. 123.]

℣. Ascendo ad patrem meum et patrem vestrum

The Sonday wtin the vtas.

NOn relinquam vos . . . cor uestrum alleluya alleluya [Y. 187.]

℣. Nisi abiero . . mittam eum ad vos.

Et. [Y. 187.]

O rex glorie . . . spiritum veritatis alleluia. [S. B. i. dccccIxv.]

℣. Ascendo ad patrem et patrem vestrum.

[1] *written in margin in red.*

On witsonday procession. Sedit angelus *withowt the verse. antym.*

HOdie completi . . . saluus erit alleluia.
℣. Spiritus sanctus procedens a throno. [S. 125.]

On Trinite Sonday this procession.

SUmme trinitati . . . orbem legibus. [S. 125.]
℣. Prestet nobis . . . almi. Qui. [S. 125.]

HOnor virtus . . . tempore. [S. 126.]
℣. Trinitati lux perhennis vnitati sit decus perpetim. In perhenni. [S. 126.]
℣. Verbo domini celi firmati sunt.

In the fest of corporis xpi thys procession. ℟.

EGo sum panis vite patres vestri manducauerunt manna in deserto & mortui sunt. Hic est panis de celo descendens si quis ex ipso manducauerit non morietur.
℣. Ego sum panis viuus qui de celo descendi siquis manducauerit ex hoc pane uiuet ineternum. Hic est.
℣. Panem de celo prestitisti eis.

The Sonday within the vtas of corporis xpi. this Responsory.

REspexit helias . . . ad montem dei. [S. 127.]
℣. Si quis . . . in eternum. Et ambulauit. [S. 128.]
℣. Panem de celo.

On seynt Iohn baptist euen procession.

INnuebant patri eius quem vellet vocari eum et postulans pugillarem scripsit dicens. Iohannes est nomen eius.
℣. Apertum est os zacharie & prophetauit dicens. Iohannes.
℣. ffuit homo missus.

*On the Day of S^t. Ioh*n. *bap*tist. *this pro*cession.

INter natos mulierum non surrexit maior iohanne baptista. Qui viam domino preparauit in heremo.
℣. Fuit homo missus a deo cui nomen iohannes erat.

The sonday within the vtas. ℟

INnuebant.

PRo eo quod non credidisti verbis meis eris tacens & non poteris loqui vsque in diem natiuitatis eius.

℣. ffuit homo missus.

On yͤ sonday within the vtas of peter & paule this ℟.

ISti sunt due oliue. . . . facte sunt. [S. B. iii. 353.]

℣. In omnem terram . . . eorum. Quia. [S. B. ii. 365.]

This procession seruus on sondaies fro Deus omnium. *to Aduent.*

ORemus dilectissimi nobis deum patrem omnipotentem vt cunctis mundum purget erroribus morbos auferat famem repellat aperiat carcerem vincula dissoluat Peregrinantibus reditum infirmantibus sanitatem nauigantibus portum salutis indulgeat et pacem tribuat in diebus nostris insurgentibusque repellat inimicos et de manu inferni liberet nos propter nomen suum alleluya.

a'. Descendi in ortum meum.

℣. Post partum.

a'.

CUm venerimus ante conspectum domini in die iudicii vbi assistunt milia milium et decies centena milia angelorum archangelorum cherubyn et seraphyn. Ubi sanctorum chorus circumastat patriarcharum ac prophetarum apostolorum et martirum & omnia agmina sanctorum quia ibi iudicium in quo sine testibus omnia manifesta sunt.

a'. Beata dei genitrix.

℣. Post partum.

OMnipotens deus supplices te rogamus et petimus vt intercessio archangelorum sit pro nobis grata tibi semper. Michaelis et gabrielis pariterque et raphaelis vt digni offeramus tibi hostias ad altare et appareamus ante saluatorem per intercessionem nouem ordinum angelorum Thronorum et dominacionum Principatum et potestatum cum cherubyn et seraphyn vt ipsi intercedant pro nobis qui non cessant clamare dicentes Sanctus sanctus sanctus dominus deus exercituum rex israhel qui regnas sine fine dignare famulos tuos hodie exaudire alleluya.

℣. Post partum virgo.

At the first euensong of .s'. Thomas of canterbery to his .a'. ℟.

QUam pulchra quam sunt beate tua preconia tuis meritis ignis accensus extinguitur extinctus accenditur terra quos premit non opprimit ventus quiescit mare obsedit.

℣. Quoniam te fideliter subiecisti creatori ideo mirabiliter tibi seruit creatura.
℣. Ora pro nobis beate thoma.

In the Translacion of Seynt Benedicte att euensonge.

SAnctus pater benedictus
prophetie spiritu plenus.
Cepit ventura predicere
presens absencia nunciare
ac per sompnum semet exhibere.

℣. Regios euentos† pandit fratres comedentes detersit dormientibus fabricam ostendit. Cepit.

At the first euensong of seynt margaret to hir auter. ℟

REgnum mundi . . . dilexi.
℣. Eructavit . . . regi. Quem. Gloria patri et filio et spiritui sancto. [S. B. ii. 447.]

At the first euensong of seynt marie magdaleyn. ℟.
Regnum mundi.

In the vigil of seynt Iames to his auter say y^is^ .℟.

QUi sunt isti . . . suas.
versus. Candidiores niue . . antiquo. Et quasi. [Y. B. ii. 652.]

At the first euensong of seynt Anne this procession .a'.

AD felicis anne festum
omnes fluant populi
cuius proles effugauit
densam noctem seculi

dum maria maris stella
celebs nupta peperit
et per natum eius christum
mors eterna deperit

apud ipsum sint pro nobis
& mater et filia
vt in orto sponsi rosas
legamus et lilia.
℣.†

In the vigil of the Assumpcion of oure lady this .R.
Aue regina.

Ande if it fall on Sonday this .R.
O Decus uirginitatis . . . regina. [Y. 198.]
V. Accipe quod offerimus redona quod rogamus excusa quod timemus.
V. Salue stella maris memorare quibus memoraris. Mater.
V.†

In the Assumpscion of oure lady this procession.
FElix namque es sacra . . . christus deus noster.
V. Ora pro populo . . . assumptionem. Quia. [S. 154.]

If it fall on a sonday then this .a'. shall be saide
Hodie maria.
V. Exaltata es sancta.

The sonday within ye vtas ye shal say this O decus.
HOdie[1] . . . in eternum. [S. B. iii. 700.]
V. Exaltata es sancta dei. [S. 154.]

In the natiuite of o^r lady this procession .R.
SOlem iusticie . . . ortum.
V. Cernere . . . fideles. Stella. Gloria . sancto. Stella [S. B. iii. 781.]
V. Elegit eam deus.

If it fall on a sonday this shall be saide.
NAtiuitas tua . . . vitam sempiternam. [S. 156.]

The Sonday withine the vtas.
Solem iusticie.

In ye Exultacion of the cros y^is .R.
CRux benedicta . . . nostra lauit alleluya alleluya. [S. B. iii. 823.]
V. Corpore quidem in ligno pependit pro uulnere nostro. Atque. Gloria patri et filio et spiritui sancto. Atque.

[1] *The anthem* Hodie *is repeated and the arrangements confused.*

In the vigil of all halowes to yᵉ auter yˢ. ℟

SInt lumbi vestri . . . reuertatur a nuptiis.
℣. Vigilate ergo . . . venturus sit. Et. Gloria patri et filio et spiritui sancto. Et. [S. B. iii. 974.]
℣. Orate pro nobis omnes sancti dei.

On the day this procession.

COncede nobis . . . societatem.
℣. Adiuuent nos . . . peccati. [Y. 199.]
℟ Sint lumbi.

Of seynt Edmund to his auter thys .℟.

MIles christi gloriose
edmunde sanctissime.
Tuo pio interuentu
Culpas nostras ablue.
℣. Ut celestis regni sedem . . .
valeamus scandere. Tuo. Gloria patri et filio et spiritui sancto. Culpas. [Y. 201.]

Of seynt katherine

ANima mea . . . amore langueo. Amen. [S. B. iii. 685.]

In the visitacion of oʳ lady ℟.

O mater montem saliens
fuisti virga† vigilans
angelo precedente.
Ad mentes contemplancium
regendas† ex aromatum
fragore† defluente.
℣. Ibi flos campi filia†
velut conuallis lilia
nitorem dat in mente. Ad. Gloria patri et filio et spiritui sancto. Ad mentes.

In the comyng in the chirche say thys antym.

CArisma sancti spiritus
diffudit se diuinitus
in puerum cum sensit
verbum salutiferum
marie sibi obuium
elisabeth accensit.
℣. Elegit eam deus et preelegit

In the dedicacion of the chirche say this procession .℟.

TErribilis est . . . loco isto et ego nesciebam.
℣. Cunque euigilasset iacob quasi de graui somno ait. Vere.
Gloria patri et filio et spiritui sancto. Vere.

In comyng in to the chirche say

O quam metuendus est locus iste vere non est hic aliud nisi domus dei et porta celi. [S. B. i. mccccxlix.]
℣. Domus mea.

Of Saynct Benet this Responsorye.

FRater erat mente captiuus oracionis tempore uagus quem sanctus egressum virga percussit & trahentem se puerum nigrum fugauit.
℣. Qui ex illa die nil tale passus est ab hoste sed immobilis permansit in oracione. Quem.
℣. Os iusti meditabitur

QUi[1] creauit celum lully lully lu.
Nascitur in stabulo byby byby by.
Rex qui regit seculum lully lully lu.

Ioseph emit panniculum byby byby by.
Mater inuoluit puerum lully lully lu.
Et ponit in presepio byby byby by.

Inter animalia lully lully lu.
Iacent mundi gaudia byby byby by.
Dulcis super omnia lully lully lu.

Lactat mater domini. byby byby by
Osculatur paruulum lully lully lu.
Et adorat dominum byby byby by.

Roga mater filium lully lully lu.
Ut det nobis gaudium byby byby by.
In perenni gloria lully lully lu.

In sempiterna secula byby byby by.
Ineternum et vltra lully lully lu.
Det nobis sua gaudia byby byby by.
℣. Puer natus est nobis.

[1] *The carol with its music is given in collotype at the end of the volume.*

oracio.

COncede quesumus omnipotens deus . . seruitus tenet. Per eundem. [S. 14.]

On shere thursday this. antym.

DOminus iesus postquam . . . ita faciatis. [S. M. 303.]
℣. Ostende nobis domine misericordiam tuam.
Et salutare tuum.
kyrieleison. Christeleison. kyrieleison.
Pater noster.
Et ne nos.
Sed libera.
Suscepimus deus misericordiam tuam.
In medio templi tui.
Tu mandasti.
Mandata tua custodiri nimis.
Domine exaudi orationem meam.
Et clamor.
Dominus vobiscum.

oracio.

ADesto domine ihesu christe . . . omnia nostra interiora lauentur peccata quod ipse prestare digneris. Qui cum patre et spiritu sancto viuis et regnas deus per omnia secula seculorum. Amen. [S. 66.]

This payer† folowyng shalbe saide afft^r^ complen.

AUe sponsa incorrupta.
aue per quam orbis lapsi
facta est ereptio.
Aue per quam occumbentis
est ade surrectio.
Aue per quam prime matris
est eue redemptio.
Sancta maria ora pro nobis
aue sponsa incorrupta.

Altitudo cogitandi
tu in accessibilit
inuisibile profundum
angelorum oculis
karikaristo menitrotoche partine
sancta dei genitrix ora pro nobis.

Omnia portantem portans
solium imperii

tu stella demonstrans solem
sol diei[1] mistici
occidentis austro† mundi
luminis conspicui
sancta virgo virginum ora pro nobis
sancta maria incorrupta.

Incarnationis diuini†
vteris† tu sancta† es
per quam renouantur omnes
creature species
cunque† adoratur factor
et origo omnium
angelorum domina ora pro nobis
aue sponsa incorrupta.

Tu extans iniciatrix
archam† consilii
mirandorum vere christi
operum primicie
dogmatum illius extans
tu fons & inicium
celorum regina ora pro nobis
aue sponsa incorrupta.

Scala tu celestis per quam
descendit ipse deus
sponsa traducens terrena
supera celestia
tu mater innupta omni
honore superior
virgo perpetua ora pro nobis
aue sponsa incorrupta.

Demonum forte lamentum
meror & tristicia
angelorum et bonorum
laus decus & gloria
electorum tu cunctorum
facta es leticia
templum domini ora pro nobis
aue sponsa incorrupta.

Generans perennem zepher-
um in accessibilem

[1] *The first* i *of this word is interlined.*

inuisibile super ascendens
omnium scienciam
animarum tu sanctarum
splendor et prudencia
sacrarium spiritus sancti ora pro nobis
aue sponsa incorrupta.

Cenicam† vite coronam
fructu ventris germinans
possidens diuinitatem
et in ea pullulas†
nutricans humanitatem
et eam agricolans
tu sola sine exemplo ora pro nobis
Aue sponsa incorrupta.

And there say yor. Pater noster. *as the vse is.*
Adoramus te christe &.
and. Ingressus angelus.
and. Aue maria.
and Gaude dei genitrix virgo immaculata
gaude que
gaudium ab angelo suscepisti
gaude que genuisti eterni luminis claritatem†
gaude mater gaude sancta dei genitrix uirgo
tu sola mater innupta
te laudat omnis factura
genitricem lucis
sis pro nobis quesumus perpetua interuentrix.
and Ave regina celorum aue domina . semper christum exora [S. B. iii. 784.]
a' Salue regina
With the fyue versus. and then thys antym.
Alma redemptoris mater . . . peccatorum miserere. [S. B. i. mclxix.]
and then this .℟.
Aspice domine de sede sancta . . . tribulacionem nostram. [S. B. i. mccclxxvi.]
℣. Non enim in . . . . tuis multis Aperi. [S. B. i. mccclxxx.]
kyrieleison. christeleison. kyrieleison.
Pater noster.
Et ne nos.
Sed libera.
Benedicamus patrem et filium cum sancto spiritu.
Laudemus et superexaltemus eum in secula.

Adoramus te christe & benedicimus tibi.
Quia per sanctam crucem tuam redemisti mundum.
Emitte spiritum tuum & creabuntur.
Et renouabis faciem terre.
Post partum uirgo.
Dei genitrix.
Orate pro nobis omnes sancti dei.
Ut digni efficiamur promissionibus christi.
Exurge domine adiuua nos.
Et libera nos propter nomen tuum.
Domine exaudi oracionem meam.
Et clamor.

of the trinite.
oracio.

Famulos tuos quesumus . . . regnas deus. Per. [W. iii. 1354.]

of the crosse

Deus qui sanctam crucem ascendisti . . illuminare dignare. Per christum. [S. B. ii. 92.]

Of the holy goste. Oracio.

Deus qui corda fidelium . consolacione gaudere. [S. B. i mviii.]

Of oure Lady. Oracio.

Deus qui de beate marie . adiuuemur. [S. B. ii. 90.]

Of all halows. Oracio.

Omnium sanctorum tuorum sempiterna concede. [S. B. ii. 93.]

For the pease. Oracio.

Deus a quo sancta . . . protectione tranquilla [S. B. ii. 254.]

of the kyng. oracio.

Quesumus omnipotens deus . valeat peruenire. [S. M. 785.*]

For the deede. Oracio.

QUesumus domine pro tua pietate . . partem restitue. [S. M. 875.*]

for the dede. oracio.

Inclina domine aurem tuam . . esse consortes. [S. M. 876.*]

oracio.

PResta quesumus domine ut animam famuli tui sacerdotis quam in hoc seculo commorantem sacris altaribus decorasti :/ in celesti sede gloriosa semper exultet.

Oracio.

Deus qui nos patrem et matrem . . fac videre. [S. M. 873.*]

Oracio.

Deus uenie largitor . . . peruenire concedas. [W. ii. 1172.]

Oracio.

Deus in cuius miseratione . . . sine fine letentur. [S. M. 877.*]

oracio.

Miserere quesumus domine . . . in celis. [S. M. 877.*]

oracio.

Fidelium deus omnium conditor . . supplicacionibus consequantur. [S. M. 879.*]

This shalbe said euery nyght afftur antym. oracio.

OMnipotens sempiterne deus qui diuina gabrielis salutacione. & sancta filii tui natiuitate. et gloriosa eius resurrectione. et admiranda eiusdem ascensione. & ueneranda genitricis ipsius assumpcione sancte marie matri tue gaudia contulisti presta quesumus :/ vt pro eius amore ab omni specie doloris et angustie liberemur et sempiternis gaudiis perfrui mereamur.

Afftur complen. oracio.

Tribue quesumus domine omnes sanctos . . . exaudire digneris. Qui tecum viuit & regnat. [S. B. ii. 93.]

Anime famulorum famularum et anime omnium fidelium defunctorum per misericordiam dei in pace requiescant. Amen.

Of the cros. oracio.

Deus qui pro nobis filium tuum . . . in resurrectionis eius gaudiis semper viuamus. [S. M. 286.]

Of oure lady. oracio

Prosit nobis semper omnipotens pater et in celo regnanti. [W. iii. 1358.]

of owre lady. oracio

Deus qui salutis eterne . filium tuum. Qui tecum. [S. B. ii. 91.]

Att matens benediccones.

Meritis et precibus beatissime dei genitricis virginis marie & omnium sanctorum saluet & benedicat nos omnipotens & misericors dominus. Amen.

Benedictione perpetua :' benedicat nos pater eternus.

Deus dei filius :' nos benedicere et adiuuare dignetur.

Spiritus sancti gracia :' illuminet corda et corpora nostra.

Omnipotens dominus sua gracia nos benedicat.

In Secundo nocturno.

Exaudi christe preces nostras qui cum patre et spiritu sancto viuis & regnas deus per omnia secula seculorum.

Ad gaudia paradisi :' perducat nos misericordia christi.

Intus & exterius :' nos purget spiritus almus.

Sancte trinitatis clemencia :' det nobis uite et perennis gaudia.

Ad gaudia polorum ducat nos rex angelorum.

In .iii.º Nocturno.

Adiutorium nostrum in nomine domini :' qui fecit celum et terram.

Per euangelica dicta :' deleantur nostra delicta.

Diuinum auxilium ꝫ maneat semper nobiscum.

Ad societatem ciuium supernorum ꝫ perducat nos rex angelorum.

Deus misereatur nostri ꝫ & det nobis suam pacem.

In feriis eciam in festis of .iii. lessons.

Ostende nobis domine misericordiam tuam.

Ardeat in nobis ꝫ diuina† ferueat† amoris.

In vnitate sancti spiritus ꝫ benedicat nos pater & filius.

Christus perpetue ꝫ det nobis gaudia vite.

Of owre lady benesons.

Precibus et meritis.

Mater misericordie ꝫ aperiat nobis ianuam celestis glorie.

Regina celestis ꝫ succurre nobis miseris.

Alma virgo virginum ꝫ intercede pro nobis ad dominum.

Sancte marie intercessio ꝫ fiat peccatorum nostrorum remissio.

In .ii.º Nocturno.

Exaudi christe preces n[ostras].

Stella maria maris ꝫ succurre piissima nobis.

Crimina nostra purga[1] ꝫ pia mater virgo maria.

[1] pia *was written first and afterwards altered.*

Sancta maria cum filio suo ȝ nos benedicere et adiuuare dignetur.

In omni tribulatione & angustia ȝ succurre nobis virgo maria.

In .iii.º Nocturno.

Adiutorium nostrum.

Per beate marie merita ȝ prosit nobis leccio euangelica.

Ab illo mereamur benedici ȝ qui de virgine dignatus est nasci.

Ihesus marie filius ȝ sit nobis clemens et propicius.

In mortis hora ȝ succurre nobis. virgo maria.

of oʳ lady an''

Beata dei genitrix . . . femineo sexu. [S. B. iii. 784.]
Descendi in ortum . . . intueamur te. [S. B. iii. 685.]
Virgo hodie fidelis . . . in mulieribus. [S. B. i. cxcvi.]
[A blank which the rubricator has not filled up.]

Rex seculorum quem laudat vniuersa substancia rerum per te creatarum exaudi[te] fantes et tui benedicti festo iubilantes quos erutos a crimine facias secum† viuere. christe salus nostra christe finis expectacionis nostre.

In regeneracione cum sederit filius . . . tribus israhel. [S. B. ii. 371.]

Dominica infra octavam corporis christi .a'.

O sacrum conuiuium . . . pignus datur allcluya. [S. 128.]

Maria virgo semper letare
que meruisti cristum portare
celi et terre conditorem
quia de tuo vtero protulisti mundi saluatorem.

Auc o theotecos†
virgo maria virgo fuisti
et in virginitate permansisti
dei genitrix intercede pro nobis.

Aula maria dei casta titulusque pudoris
porta syon rutilans rutilis fundata saphiris
que sola cunctis patuisti clausa tonanti
suscipe seruorum miserans pia vota tuorum.

A Deuote prayer.[1]

O blessed ihū hyghe heuens kynge
I moste Synfull creature of all lyuyng.
O maker of nyght and day.
hertely lorde I the pray.
That I may loue the ouer all thynge.
O ihū ihū swete ihū
thy loue in me synnar so renew.
that it may be aboue all mesure.
and on the to sett all my tresure.
ffor so ought to love the. o. ihū.
And all vices for thy sake to esshewe.
O dere Jhū all the ioy of my Sowle.
Bren my hertt Jhū as fyre dothe the cole.
that noo thynge lake I beseche the.
which belongethe to p*er*fite charite.
O mercyfull Jhū the sykyr stoone.
of charite is in the alone.
And whoo soo may haue it throghe thy pyte.
He is full sykur to dwell with the.
O dere worthe Jhū I beseche the also.
that I may loue my neyghbur as I shuld doo.
Euen as my selff. doo he me goode or ylle.
ffor thy loue lorde and for non oy*er* skyll.
O myghtffull ihū I beseche thy grace.
That I may hate deedly Synne in eu*ery* place.
And specially for thy loue and for noo feere.
of payne nodre here nor ells where.
O Jhū the wysdome of the trinite:
yf I myght the loue Jhū brennyngly.
The dreede of dethe myght neuer perce myn hertt.
nor the greate paynes of hell that ben so smertt.
O Jhū the lampe in whoome is all lyght.
thy loue is soo co*m*fortable in the goostly syght.
That all derke clowdes of dreede ben cleene chacede away.
If we lorde in thy loue study myght.
O moste meeke Jhū and mercyfull kynge.

[1] *Here the character of the writing changes from a liturgical to an ordinary hand.*

Gyve me grace Jhū yf it be thy lykynge.
Gladly to couett for thy loue to dye.
And to be gladd for thy loue to suffre all envy.
O mercifull Jhū to thy louers all.
O swete derlynge to the sowle that on the dothe call.
O verey godd. O verey man that all thynge hathe wroght
haue mercy on me A Synnar. thoue hathe me deere boght.
Amen.

A praier to the goode Angell.

O swete angell to me soo deere.
that nyght and day standithe me neere.
ffull loueyngly with mylde moode.
Thankyng. loueyng. loue & praysyng.
Offer for me to Jhū ōr kyng.
ffor his gyfftes greate and goode.
As thow gothe betwix hym and me.
And knowethe my lyffe in euery degre.
Saying it in his presence.
Aske me grace to loue hym truly.
To serue my lorde with hertt duly.
With my dayly diligence.
Keepe me from vice and all perells.
Whiles thowe wt me dayly trauells.
In this worlde of wyckednesse.
Sett me my peticions grauntede.
By thy praier dayly haunted.
Yff it please thy holynes.

The versicull.

O swete Angell that keepithe me :/
Bryng me to blysse I pray the.

The collect.

O my lorde Jhū crist as it hathe pleasede the to Assigne an Angell to wayte on me dayly and nyghtly with greate attendance and diligence soo I beseche the throghe his goyng betwix vs. that thow clense me frome vyces. clethe me wt vertues graunt me loue and grace to come see and haue wtowte ende thy blysse before thy faire face that lyueth and regnethe afftur thy gloriouse passion wt the ffader of heuen. and wt the holy gooste one godd and persones three with owte ende in blysse. Amen.

A deuoute prayer.

O Jhū to all thy true louers.
Graunt peace of hert and stedffast mynde :
To theym that y^i loue dothe seke.
Thou graunt theym thy grace and solas eke.
O ffader dere moste of powere.
Gyff thy children thy loue in fere.
And grace to keepe the same.
O Jhū flowre moste of honor.
O swete sapowre moste of dulcoure.
Blessed be thy name.
O spirit inspire loue and desire.
Accende thy ffyre.[1]
defende frome ire.
And keepe vs frome blame.
O Lady bryght
launterne of lyght.
Swettist wyght
moder of myght.
And mayden of goode fame.
O true loue true knytt in vertue.
Thy loue to grow in vs euerr newe.
Gyff vs grace withoute reclame.
O blessed mary v*ir*gyn of nazareth.
And moder of almyghty lorde of grace.
Which his peple saued hase.
deth frome the paynes of the infernall place.
Now blessed lady kneele afore his face.
And pray hym soone my sowle to saue from losse
which with hys blessed bloode bought hase.
throw hyt greate passion nailed on the crosse.
Amen.

A goode praier.

O Jhū lett me neuer forgett thy byttr passion
That thou suffred for my transgression.
For in thy blessyd wondes is the verey scole.
That must teche me wt the worlde to be called a ffole.
O Jhū ihū ihū grauntt that I may loue the soo.
Yt the wysdom of the worlde be cleene fro me A goo.
And brennyngly to desyre to come to see thy face.
In whome is all my comford my ioy and my solace.
¶ Amen—Jh*esus*—maria—Joh*anne*s.

[1] *This line is written a little larger than the others.*

O Swete ihū gyve me thy loue and grace for to keepe thy co*m*maundments. *Pater noster. Aue maria.*

O swete Jhū gyve me grace for thy loue to dreede hate and flee synne. *Pater noster. Aue maria.*

O Swete Jhū thy precious bloodc ande thy byttur passion be my redempcion and saluacion. *Pater noster. Aue maria.*

O Swete Jhū haue mercy of all the soules in purgatory. and saue me fro*m* hell. *Pater noster. Aue maria.*

O Swete Jhū when shall I see thy gloriouse face with all thy blessed Sayntes in ioy wᵗoute ende. Amen. *Pater noster. Aue maria & Credo.*

O Gloriouse Jhū. O mekest Jhū. O moste swettest Jhū. I pray the. that I may haue trew confession. contricion and satisfacion or I dye. And that I may see and receyve thy holy bodye godd and man Sauyoʳ of all mankynd Crist Jhū with owte synne. And that thow wilt my lorde godd forgyve me all my synnes ffor thy gloriouse wondes and passion. And that I may ende my lyffe in the trew ffeyth of holy churche. and in p*er*fite loue and charite wᵗ my euen cristen as thy creature. And I co*m*maund my sowle in to thy holy hand*e*s throgh the glorious helpp of thy blessed moder of mercy oure lady saynt marie. and all the holy company of heuen. The holy body of crist ihū be my saluacion of body and soule. Amen. The gloriose bloode of cryst Jhū bryng my sowle and body in to the euer lastynge blysse. Amen. I cry godde mercy. I cry godde mercy. I cry godde mercy. Welcome my maker. Welcome my redemer. Welcome my Sauyoure. I cry the m*er*cy with hertt contrite of my greate vnkyndnesse that I haue hadd to the. Amen.

A goode praier.

O the moste swetest spouse of my sowle c*r*iste Jhū desyryng heretely euer more for to be with the in mynde and wyll. and to lett noo erthly thyng be soo nygh myn hertt as the c*r*iste Jhū. And that I dreede nott for to dye for to goo to the criste Jhū. And that I may euer more say to the wᵗ a gladd cheere. my Lord my godd my souereigne Sauyoure crist Jhū. I besche yᵉ hertely take me Synnar vnto thy greate m*er*cy and grace. For I loue the with all myn hertt wᵗ all my mynde. and wʰ all my myght. and nothy*n*g so myche in erthe nor aboue the erthe as I doo the my swete Lord crist Jhū. And for yᵗ I haue nott loued the. nor worshipped the aboue all thyngˢ as my lord my god and my Sauyoure criste Jhū I beseche the with mekenes and hert contrite of mercy and of forgevenes of my greate vnkyndenes for the greate loue that thowe shewdest for me and all mankynd what tyme thow offredest thy glorious body god and man vnto the crosse ther to be crucified ande wounded. and vnto thy glorious hertt a sharp spere. there rennyng oute plentuously blode and water for the redempcion and saluacion of me and all mankynde. And thus hauyng reme*m*brau*n*ce stedfastly in my hert of the my sauyour cryste Jhū I dowtt not but thow wylt be full nyghe me and comfort me both bodely and gostely w^{t} thy glorious presens. And at the last. bryng me vnto thyn eu*er*lastyng blysse the whiche shall neu*er* haue ende. Amen.

Carmen. xpo Jhū.

Jesu swete now wyll I syng :/
To the A song of love longyng.
Doo in myn hert a well to spryng.
The to loue ouer all thyng :/

Jhū swete my hertye lyght :/
Thow art day withoute nyght.
Gyve me grace of gostely lyght :/
and the to love with all my myght :/

Jhū swete my sowle bote.
In my hertt thow sett a roote :/
of thy love that is so swete :/
and wete it lord that it grow myght.

Jhū godd thy love is swete.
woo is to hym that itt shall lete :/
gyve me grace lorde for to weepe.
For my synnes terys wete.

Jhū swete well may he bee :/
that the shall in thy ioye see :/
with loue cordys draw thow me :/
that I co*m*me and dwell w^{t} the.

Jhū thy loue to vs was so free :/
that it fro*m* heuen broght the :/
for love thow dere boght me :/
ffor loue thow hangest on the roode tree.

Jhū for loue thow suffredest woo :/
that blody stremys dyd renne the ffroo :/

thy white body was blacke and bloo.
Oure synnes it made so weyle A woo.

Jhũ thy Crowne satt full soore :'
and thy scowrgynge when thow bett wore :'
yt was for me ihũ thyne oore :'
the paynes that thow suffred thoore.

Jhũ swete thow honge on tree :'
not for thy gylt but for me :'
ffor synnes I dyd ageynst the :'
Swete ihũ forgive theym me.

Jhũ what sawe thow in me :'
Of ought that nedefull was to the :'
that thow soo hard on roode tre :'
woldes for me so payned be.

Jhũ why was thow iolyouse :'
Soo feruent and soo coryouse :'
To bye w^{t} pryce so preciouse :'
wretchyd man soo viciouse.

Jhũ my god my lord my kyng :'
ffor itt askethe noone other thyng :'
Butt true hertt in loue longyng :'
And loue terys with styll mowrnyng :'

Mary lady moder bryght :'
thow darst thow wylt. thow artt of myght :'
My hert my loue my lyffe my lyght :'
thow pray for vs bothe day and nyght.

Jhũ thy loue is all my thoght :'
of other thyng rech I ryght noght :'
But I haue ageynst the wroght :'
And thow me hathe soo deere boght :'

ffull longe lord thow haste spared me :'
the more ought I to loue the :'
That thow w^{t} me hathe ben soo ffree :'
And I A trayto^{r} ageynst the.

Jhũ of loue I see tokennyng :'
thyne armes spred to lo clyppyng :'

thy heede bowede to swete kyssynge :'
thy syde opened to loue shewyng :'

Jhū euer when I thynk on the :'
and looke vp on thy roode tre.
Thy swete body blody I se :'
lorde doo that syght to wounde me.

Jhū thy moder yt by the stoode :'
on loue terys she lete a ffloode.
Thy woundys and thy holy bloode :'
made hyre full of drury moode.

Jhū loue the dyd to grete :'
loue the dyd thy lyne to swete :'
ffor loue thow was ful soore a bete :'
loue the dyd thy lyffe to lete.

Mary yt slakyst all woo :'
hell paynes kepe vs froo :'
And gyve vs grace here to do soo :'
yt we frome hens to heuen goo :'

Jhū wells fynde I in the :'
yt to loue spryng myght draw me :'
of reede blode the stremys be :'
My sowle eu*en* washe ye.

Jhū my sowle draw ye to :'
make my hertt wyde vndo :'
gyve it thy loue to drynke so :'
that fleshly lustys ben fordo :'

Jhū make me loue the so :'
that where I be or what I do :'
that I for weele or for woo :'
let neuer my hertt turne the froo.

Jhū my weyle and all my wyn :'
all my ioy is the within :'
Now and euer kepe me frome syne :'
To do thy wyll lett me nott blyn.

Jhū myghtfull heuen kyng :'
thy loue be all my lykyng :'

My mowrnyng and my longyng :'
w^t swete terys gretyng :'

Jhũ gyve me grace y^t I may see :'
thy greate goodenes done to me :'
and I vnkynde ageyn haue be :'
fforgyve me lorde y^t artt so fre :'

Jhũ thy loue and ffleshly thoght :'
won to gedre y^ai may noght :'
as hony and gall to gedre broght :'
Swete and bytt^r accordeth noght.

Jhũ thoghe I be vnworthy :'
the to loue lorde almyghty :'
y^i goodenes makethe me hardy :'
My sowle to doo In thy mercy.

Jhũ thy mercy comfortes me :'
ffor no man may soo synfull be :'
y^t synne wyll leyue and turne to me :'
But mercy and grace ffyndes he.

Mary mylde pray for me :'
to thy dere son ffull of pety :'
y^t he grauntt me to be :'
Euer in blysse with hym and the.

Jhũ thow helpe at myn endyng :'
take my sowle at my dyinge.
Send it socowr and comfortyng :'
y^t it dreede noo wycked thyng.

Amen for charite.

[1]This booke longeth to
Dame Margery
Byrkenhed of[2]
Chestre[1]

[1]—[1] *This is written in a hand like the first part of the book.*
[2] f *has been partly erased.*

Ego[1] precor dominum nostrum Iesum christum et dulcissimam matrem suam sanctam mariam atque sanctum benedictum patronum nostrum[2] necnon omnes sanctos celi et vos dominam meam. dominam priorissam et conventum vestrum quatinus dignemini recipere me in vestram societatem et concedere michi habitum vestrum pro sancta caritate.

Omnipotens[3] sempiterne deus nos famulos tuos dextera potencie tue a cunctis protege periculis et beata maria semper virgine intercedente cum omnibus sanctis tuis fac nos presenti gaudere prosperitate et futura per.

[1] *This is written in a different hand at bottom of pag*
[2] *interlined.*
[3] *This is written on a flyleaf.*

NOTES.

p. 1.

De te virgo] This is an anthem of the Blessed Virgin proper for Advent. It was sung at compline by the Brigittine nuns during Advent up to the compline of Christmas Eve inclusive. It is spoken of as: "*A Complie la louange.* De te Virgo." The following text of the anthem is taken from their printed breviary:

Haec Antiphona cum Versiculo & Collecta sequenti dicitur ab Aduentu Domini vsque ad festum Natiuitatis eiusdem.

De te Virgo nasciturum mundi Saluatorem patres suspirauerunt, praedixerunt Prophetae, signauerunt figurae, tandem ille paranymphus caelestis Gabriel salutando nunciauit, Spiritus sanctus obumbrando foecundauit. O quando veniet ille desideratus! O quando ex te nascetur diu expectatus! Veni, veni Domine, iam veni, per viscera Virginis visitans nos oriens ex alto. (*Breviarium Sororum ac Sancti monialium sacri ordinis divae Brigittae, &c.* Atrebati, Robertus Maudhuy, 1610, p. 298.)

This corresponds with the text of the anthem in the Syon manuscript in the Library of Magdalene College, Cambridge, G. 14. 11. fo. 81.

Quomodo fiet] S.B. i. cxix.

Rorate caeli] S.B. i. cxviii.

Note 1.

Et nunc sequimur] W. Maskell, *Monumenta ritualia Ecclesiae Anglicanae*, Oxford, 1882, iii. 342.

Amo Christum] W. Maskell, *op. cit.* p. 340. W. iii. 1198.

Verbum Patris] Respond and Versicle to fourth lesson at Mattins of the Conception in *Breviarium Aberdonense*, pars hyemalis, London, 1854, ed. W. J. Blew, *verbatim* as in text. ℟. and ℣. to ninth lesson of Conception in *Breviarium Halberstad.* Nurnberge, Georg. Stuchs, 1515. to seventh lesson in *Breviarium Patavien.* Venetiis, P. Liechtenstein, 1508. to fifth lesson in *Breviarium Trevirense*, Francof. et Treviris, 1748. pars hyemalis.

F. J. Mone (*Lateinische Hymnen*, Freiburg in Breisgau, 1854, ii. 10) has printed the whole of the anthems and responds in verse, of which this *Verbum patris* is a part. It was printed also by Ant. de Balinghem. (*Parnassus marianus*, Duaci, 1624. p. 14.) The Halberstadt breviary reads *Ut super vellus*, with the text; Mone and the Triers breviary have *Sicut in vellus;* Passau reads: *Et sicut in:* and *tonus* instead of *onus* in the line above.

p. 2.

Hic est discipulus] S.B. i. ccxvii & ccxv.

p. 3.

Rex magnus] Respond to seventh lesson of Sunday within the octave of Epiphany in Durham Breviary. (Brit. Mus. MS. Harl. 4664. fo. 39.)

Et intrantes.] S.B. i. cccxxxviii.

O Maria Iesse virga] Anthem for Sunday within the octave of the Epiphany in *Processionale ordinis S. Benedicti*, Rothomagi, D. du Petit Val, 1623, p. 43. It occurs also in Bianchini's folio edition of Thomasius (*Opera*, Romae, 1741. I. ii. 493.) among the *Antiphonae dominicales, et ad processionem* at Christmas time. There are verbal variations from the text in both. In the second line instead of *iam olim promissum florem* the Benedictine processional has *iam florem aeterni fructus*. In the fourth line the Benedictine book has *sentiamus te piam et singulari;* where Bianchini has *sentiamus et piam et singularis.* At Cluny *O Maria* was sung after *O beata infantia* on Christmas Day and apparently up to Candlemas. ([Marquard Herrgott,] *Vetus Disciplina Monastica*, Parisiis, 1726. pp. 289 & 297.)

Virgo hodie fidelis] S.B. i. cxcvi.

On candlemas day] None of the prayers accompanying the blessing of the candles is given. We have merely the anthems sung at the procession; and these are the same as those in the Sarum book, saving *Cum inducerent;* which, however, is in the Sarum breviary as a respond to the seventh lesson on this day. (S.B. iii. 141.) Mr. Birkbeck notes variations in the music of *Cum inducerent* from that of Sarum.

p. 4.

Simeon iustus] S.B. iii. 137.

We may note an octave to Candlemas. The nuns of Syon had the same. (See MS. in Magdalene College, Cambridge, G. 14. 11. fo. ff. 14. & 15*b*.)

Hodie Maria] Anthem to *Magnificat* at second evensong of Candlemas at Durham. (Brit. Mus. Harl. 4664. fo. 213*b*.)

Christe pater] This anthem is to be found in Bianchini's edition of Thomasius. (*op. cit.* p. 493.) It is the first *Antiphona in Quadragesima.*

In last line but one read *confundamur.*

Christe pater was sung alternately with *Cum sederit* at Cluny at procession from the first Sunday of Lent to Easter. (Herrgott, *op. cit.* p. 303.)

Anima mea] S. 131.

Descendi in hortum] S. 131.

Beata Dei genetrix] S. 130.

Post partum Virgo] S.B. ii. 515.

O felix Benedicte] Respond after the ninth lesson on the feast of the Translation of St. Benedict, in the Durham Breviary. (Brit. Mus. Harl. 4664. fo. 242.)

p. 5.

Os iusti.] S.B. ii. 541.

Dederunt in escam meam fel] S.B. i. dccxiv.

Descendi in hortum meum] S. 131.

On passion Sunday] Here is evidence that the English called the fifth Sunday in Lent Passion Sunday. But they did not call the following week Passion week. That was the name for the week before Easter. See *Transactions of the London and Middlesex Archæological Society*, 1881. v. 337. where "a harrow for tenebris Candles, in passhon weke" at St. Stephen Walbrook in 1558. is spoken of. Also in *the Pylgrymage of Sir Richard Guylforde*, Camden Society, 1851. p. 1. which was in 1506. they took ship on "the Wednysday at nyght in Passyon weke . . . . and the nexte daye, that was Shyre Thursdaye."

In a Christchurch, Canterbury, manuscript (Harl. 2892. fo. 54*b*.) the Monday in Holy Week is spoken of as *feria ii. de passione domini.*

On palm Sunday] As at Candlemas, there is no form for blessing the palms, and the anthems and hymns are all to be found in the Sarum book, though all the Sarum forms are not here. They also follow very much the same order.

I have no suggestions to make as to the place of the "city of Jerusalem." It is entered directly after the anthem *Cum appropinquaret* is sung, which describes our Lord's entry into Jerusalem; and in the Sarum book an anthem beginning *Hierusalem* (S. 50.) is sung immediately before *En rex venit*, which in the text the prioress and two ladies proclaim from Jerusalem.

The nuns are called "ladies," being Benedictines, and thus "Dominae"; just as a Benedictine monk is "Dominus," Dom, or Dan.

p. 6.

Salve lux] S. has *Salve rex.*

Cum appropinquaret.] The most usual gospel is *Cum appropinquasset* from St. Matthew (xxi. 1–9.) the Sarum gospel for the first Sunday in Advent. *Cum appropinquarent* is the usual reading of St. Mark (xi. 1,) and it is also that in Tib. c. 1. fo. 99. where it is the gospel for the blessing of the palms. With the anthem *Cum appropinquaret* just before, the scribe might very well confuse the beginning of the gospel with the anthem; and later on we shall find evidence that he was not always extremely careful in what he wrote.

It may be noted that the gospel is sung on the north half of the high cross in the churchyard.

On Shere Thursday] The directions for the washing of the altars on Shere Thursday give us a list of the altars in the church. They seem to have been thirteen in number, five being dedicated in honour of women saints, and one of All Hallows.

p. 7.

Iohannes apostolus] S.B. i. ccxv.

O beate Iacobe] I have been unable to find this anthem.

Beatus Nicolaus] S.B. iii. 36.

Non est inventus] S.B. ii. 419.

Dei repletus gratia] First anthem at lauds on the feast of the translation of St. Benedict in Durham Breviary (Harl. 4664. fo. 242.)

p. 8.

Erat autem] Mr. Dewick points out to me that this anthem is found in the Sarum *Horae.* (*Horae Beatissimae Virginis* &c. Paris. F. Regnault, 1530. fo. xxv. *b.*)

Ego sum pastor.] S.B. i. dccccxcv.

In bello victus] I have not found this anthem elsewhere.

Anna deo vigilavit] Neither anthem nor collect have I been able to find elsewhere.

Magdalenam sua crimina] I have not found this elsewhere.

Elizabeth Zachariae] S.B. iii. 347.

p. 9.

Omnipotens sempiterne] This collect may be found in *Rituale seu Mandatum insignis Ecclesiae Suessionensis*, Suessione, 1856. ed. Poquet p. 199. It has been printed from a manuscript of the 13th century.

Gaudent in caelis] Third anthem at first evensong of All Hallows at York. (Y.B. ii. 647.)

Ave regina caelorum] S.B. iii. 784.

Mandatum novum] See the directions in Lanfranc's Constitutions, the outlines of which may be compared with these, exchanging the subprioress for the *prior claustri*, and the prioress for the abbot. (D. Wilkins, *Concilia*, Lond. 1737. i. 336.)

The anthems are nearly all to be found in S. with the exception of *Accepit Maria libram*, the text of which may be found as a ℟. and ℣. to the fourth lesson at mattins on St. Mary Magdalen's day in *Breviarium secundum ritum Candidissimi Ordinis Praemonstratensis*, Pars aestivalis, Parisiis, 1598.

p. 10.

Tellus ac aethera] This hymn has been collated with two early texts in the British Museum, one in Vespasian, D. xii. fo. 69. [formerly 67.] written in England in the eleventh century: and another in Add. MS. 19768. fo. 37*b*. [formerly page 68.] probably written at St. Gall between 961 and 972.

The text is full of variants from these manuscripts, some appearing to be scribal errors, and it has been thought best to indicate these, not by the obelus as usual, but in the notes, collating the texts. Vesp. is the symbol of Vesp. D. xii. and 19768. that of the Additional MS.

Stanza 1. line 2. in magni cena principis: Vesp. 19768.
„ „ „ 3. Quo: Vesp. pectora: Vesp. 19768.
„ „ „ 4. ferculo: Vesp. 19768.
„ 2. „ 2. potentis ad mysterium: Vesp.
potentis at misterio: 19768.

Ministerium seems a better reading than *mysterium.*

Stanza 3. line 1. A celsis: Vesp. 19768.

Here again *Excelsus* may be a better reading than *a celsis.*

Stanza 3. line 4. petens : Vesp. 19768.
,, 4. ,, 1. Pallet seruus obsequio : Vesp. 19768.
,, ,, ,, 2. dominum : Vesp. 19768.
,, ,, ,, 3. limpham : Vesp. 19768 *for* limam.
,, ,, ,, 4. cena : Vesp.
Stanza 5. line 2. figurant : Vesp. 19768.
,, ,, ,, 3. Dum summus ima baiulat : Vesp. 19768.
,, ,, ,, 4. Quid cinis servit cineri : Vesp.
Quid cinis seruet cineri : 19768.
Stanza 6. line 2. fauos : Vesp. 19768.
,, ,, ,, 3. denotat : Vesp. 19768 *for* deuota.
,, ,, ,, 4. Necis qui dolos ruminat : Vesp.
necis dolos qui ruminat : 19768.
Stanza 7. line 2. fers agno : Vesp. 19768 *for* ferago.
,, ,, ,, 3. Dans : Vesp.
,, ,, ,, 4. sordes : Vesp.
,, 8. ,, 1. Nexi soluuntur hodie : Vesp. 19768.
,, ,, ,, 2. Accordis : Vesp. 19768 *for* a corde.
,, ,, ,, 3. Unguem sacratur : Vesp. Ũnguentum sacratur : 19768 *for* ungunt sacrati.
,, ,, ,, 4. Spes unde crescat miseris : Vesp.
Spes inde datur m[i]seris : 19768.
Stanza 9. line 1. inclita : 19768.
,, ,, ,, 2. gloria : 19768.
,, ,, ,, 3. patre et sancto : Vesp. 19768.
,, ,, ,, 4. Qui nos redemit obitu : Vesp. 19768.

In *Hymnarium Sarisburiense* (Lond. 1851. p. 88 note.) the variants of certain manuscripts and editions are given. But I have been unable to find *Tellus ac aethera* in Julius A. vi. nor does George Hickes mention it in the list of hymns to be found in this manuscript. (*De antiquae literaturae septentrionalis utilitate,* Oxon. 1703. Catalogus Librorum, p. 183.)

This hymn is attributed to Flavius, first Bishop of Châlon-sur-Saône, by the Statutes of Cluny (Herrgott, *op. cit.* p. 314.) where in like manner as in the text it was sung at the washing of the feet on Maundy Thursday. It is ascribed to Flavius also in J. Julian's *Dictionary of Hymnology*, Lond. 1892, p. 1137.

The melody in the text is, Mr. W. Howard Frere informs me, that often seen in mediaeval music for the hymn at Sext, *Rector potens.*

Congregavit] These are two Roman anthems which may be found on p. 160. of the Roman Missal of 1474 edited by Dr. Lippe for this Society.

p. 11.

Ecce quam bonum is the 132nd psalm, vulgate numbering; the lesson may possibly have been from St. John's Gospel, (xiii. & xiv.) ending with *Surgite eamus hinc;* as it ends in Lanfranc's Constitutions. (Wilkins, *op. cit.* i. 337.)

The first Saturday after Pasch] The Rule of St. Benedict (chapter xxxv.) orders a washing of the feet every Saturday: Pedes vero tam ipse qui egreditur quam ille qui intraturus est omnibus lauent. (*Commentaria M. F. Antonii Perez . . . in Regulam Beatissimi Patris Benedicti*, Colon. Agripp. 1688. p. 706.) It is spoken of in the *Concordia Regularis* chap. xi. (Brit. Mus. Tib. A. III. fo. 25. see W. S. Logeman, *Anglia*, 1891. Bd. xiii. p. 440.) and Aelfric's abridgement. (Corpus Christi College, Cambridge, No. 265. fo. 261. Edited by Miss Bateman, in *Compotus Rolls of the Obedientiaries of St. Swithun's Priory, Winchester*, Hampshire Record Society, 1892. p. 192.) It is alluded to in Lanfranc's Constitutions. (D. Wilkins, *Concilia*, 1737. i. 336 & 337.)

At St. Germain des Prés in Paris they sang some of the following anthems at the weekly washing of the feet and hands; as *Mandatum novum*, *Ubi est caritas*, and *Christus descendit*. (E. Martene, *De Antiquis Monachorum Ritibus*, Lib. II. Cap. xii. § x. Bassani 1788. iv. 83.) The Saturday foot washing is said to survive in the Cistercian order, "plerisque Monasteriis etiamnum viget," and the anthem *Postquam surrexit* is then sung. (*Rituale Cisterciense*, Lirinae, 1892. p. 265.) In the text, the maundy anthems have been increased by the adding of Easter anthems, especially those relating to St. Mary Magdalen.

In hoc cognoscent] See Dr. Lippe, *op. cit.* p. 160.

Diligamus] S. 65. This anthem runs on without any separation from *Ubi est caritas*, for which see Dr. Lippe, *op. cit.* p. 159.

Iesum qui crucifixus] See Thomasius, *Opera*, Romae, 1749. ed. Vezzosi, t. iv. p. 237.

Ardens est cor] See Thomasius, *op. cit.* p. 240. This and the foregoing are among the Easter anthems.

Dum flerem] Thomasius, *op. cit.* p. 243. also at Easter.

Venit Maria] Thomasius, *op. cit.* p. 127. This is the anthem for *Benedictus* on St. Mary Magdalen's day.

p. 12.

Maria ergo unxit] S. 65.

Dicite in nationibus] S.B. iii. 281.

Ascendo ad patrem] S.B. i. dcccclxii.

p. 13.

Verbo Domini] S.B. i. mli.

Ego sum panis] This is a respond following the ninth lesson on Corpus Christi day in some early editions of the Roman Breviary; and in the Pian edition it is the respond to the sixth lesson, followed by the ℣. as in the text. (S.B. i. mlxxiii.)

Innuebant] The text varies slightly from that in S.B. iii. 347.

Inter natos] S. 148.

p. 14.

Pro eo] S.B. iii. 353. and 347.

Deus omnium] The first words of the respond to the lesson *Fuit Vir*, that is, the first lesson of the first nocturn of the first Sunday after Trinity in the Sarum Breviary. (S.B. i. mclxxiv.) *Deus omnium* has become the name of this Sunday. It has the same place in the Durham Breviary; (Harl. 4664. fo. 104.) but the Sunday is there called not the first Sunday after Trinity, but *Dominica i. post oct. pentecost.*

In the *Breviarium Monasticum*, Venetiis, apud Iuntas, 1600. 8° *Deus omnium* is, however, the respond to the second lesson on the third Sunday after Pentecost.

Oremus dilectissimi] This is one of the bidding prayers amongst the *Orationes Sollemnes* of Good Friday, with an addition of a couple of lines.

It may be found as an anthem *in diebus dominicis*, but without the addition expressed, in Vezzosi's edition of Thomasius, (v. 287.) and with the addition in Bianchini's edition of the same writer. (I. i. 490.) It was sung at Soissons at the Rogations in the thirteenth century, (*Rituale* . . . *Ecclesiae Suessionensis*, p. 149.) and by Benedictines in France at the same season in the seventeenth century. (*Processionale ordinis S. Benedicti*, Rothomagi, 1623. p. 144.)

Cum venerimus] This is printed by Bianchini (*op. cit.* p. 493. as an *Antiphona in Quadragesima.*

Omnipotens Deus] This occurs among the *Antiphonae Dominicales* of Bianchini. (*op. cit.* p. 495.) It was sung at Soissons for the Rogations. (See above.)

Quam pulchra quam] *add* sancta *after second* quam.

In Durham (Brit. Mus. MS. Harl. 4664. fo. 241.*b*) this is the respond for the seventh lesson on the translation of St. Benedict, up to the word *meritis*, where the MS. changes into: rupes manant aquas aque imitantur rupem ferrum enatat aues obedit emulus perit. The ℣. is the same as in text. The anthem in the text is plainly also one for St. Benedict, as it contains allusions to the miracles of the saint. How it comes to be used for Saint Thomas of Canterbury is not clear.

p. 15.

Sanctus pater Benedictus] Respond to sixth lesson at mattins in translation of St. Benedict at Durham (Harl. MS. 4664. fo. 241.*b*.)

In ℣. Durham has *detexit* for *detersit*.

Ad felicis Annae festum] Anthem to *Magnificat* for St. Anne's service at Durham. (British Museum MS. Harl. 4664. fo. 320.)

line 9. Durham has *christum* for *ipsum*.

p. 17.

O Mater montem] Respond to sixth lesson at Mattins on the feast of the Visitation of B.V.M. in *Breviarium Halberstad.* Nurnberge, George Stuchs, 1515.

line 2. virgo: Halber.

line 7. viola: Halber

It may be a part of *Accedunt laudes virginis.* (See below.)

Carisma sancti Spiritus] Part of the wide-spread hymn *Accedunt laudes virginis.* (See G. M. Dreves, *Analecta Hymnica Medii Aevi*, Leipzig, 1896. xxiv. 89.)

p. 18.

Frater erat] I have not found this respond elsewhere. It alludes to an incident in the life of St. Benedict. A certain monk did not pray with the others, and he was led out by a little black boy, probably a devil. On St. Benedict striking the monk with his staff, the monk became as the others.

Qui creavit] Following the music the verses should be in triplets. Compare a number of verses with a refrain to each :

Verbum patris humanatur, O, O,
Dum puella salutatur, O, O,
Salutata fecundatur
Viri nescia.
℟ Ey, Ey, Eya,
Nova gaudia ! &c., &c.

(G. M. Dreves, *Analecta Hymnica Medii Aevi*, xx. 104.)

p. 19.

Dominus Iesus] This anthem is noted ; but after this musical notes cease until *Beata Dei genetrix* on p. 25.

Ave sponsa incorrupta] This is a hymn attributed to St. Anselm of Canterbury by the Benedictines, (*S. Anselmi . . . opera*, Lut. Paris. 1721. Sec. ed. Gabrielis Gerberon, p. 308.) and an earlier edition. (*Divi Anselmi Archiepiscopi Cantuariensis Opera . . .* studio et opera D. Ioannis Picardi, Coloniae Agrippina, 1612. t. iii. fo. [viii.]) Both editions read : *Ave sponsa insponsata ;* which is a refrain to many of the stanzas ; and Mr. Henry Jenner has called my attention to its identity with the refrain in the *Akathistos* of the Eastern Church, χαῖρε Νύμφη ἀνύμφευτε (Ὡρολόγιον τὸ μέγα, Rome, 1876. p. 279.) and we may notice below the introduction of a line which occurs in certain of the Greek Theotokia.

Stanza 1. line 4. *Ave . . . surrectio* not in either edition.

" 2. " 5. The editions read exactly as printed here : Χαῖρε κεχαριτομένη Θεοτόκος [Θοτόκος : Gerberon.] πάρθενη, which words begin the Theotokia for Sept. 8. Feb. 2. and other days. (Ὡρολόγιον, pp. 127. and 177.)

" 3. " 3. Both editions read : *astrum.*

" 4. " 1. Both editions read : *divae.*

2. Both editions read : *uterus tu facta* [factus : Gerberon] *es.*

3. Both editions read : *renovatur omnis,* but the reading of the text can be construed.

5. Both editions read : *cum qua,*

" 5. " 2. Both editions read : *arcani.*

" 7. " 6. Both editions read : *satians* for *facta es.*

Stanza 8. lines 1–4. Both editions have:

Generans perennem lucem
Et inaccessibilem
Sophorum superascendens
Omnium scientiam

p. 21.

Stanza 9. line 1. Read: *civicam.*
4. Read: *pullulans.*

This hymn has no musical notes, which do not appear again until *Beata Dei genetrix* on p. 25.

Adoramus te Christe] S.B. iii. 276.

Ingressus angelus] S.B. iii. 234.

Gaude Dei genetrix] This also comes from St. Anselm. (See Benedictine edition quoted above, p. 307.)

line 4. Both editions read: *charitatem*, but the reading in the text seems the better.

Salve Regina] S. 170. there followed by five verses.

p. 24.

Many of these benedictions may be found in S.B. i. signature *B.* and in Mr. Wilson's *Officium Ecclesiasticum Abbatum secundum usum Eveshamensis Monasterii*, Henry Bradshaw Society, 1893. col. 55. *Breviarium Aberdonense*, Lond. 1854. ed. W. J. Blew, after the calendar: *Portiforii seu Breviarii Sarisburiensis* fasciculus ii. Lond. 1843. p. 208.

In feriis etiam] line 2. read *divini fervor amoris*, as Mr. Wilson has suggested. This agrees more with the present text than another suggestion of *flamma*, in his edition of the Evesham book (col. 56. note). But in the Evesham book only the first letter, *f*, is given.

p. 25.

Beata Dei genetrix] These three anthems are noted.

Rex seculorum] Anthem to *Magnificat* at first evensong of the translation of St. Benedict, in the Durham Breviary. (British Museum MS. Harl. 4664. fo. 241.)

O sacrum convivium] This anthem is noted and so are the preceding from *Beata Dei.*

Maria virgo semper] This is an anthem for the assumption. It will be found among the anthems at the end of the office for this day in Thomasius, ed. Vezzosi, iv. 267; *Breviarium secundum ordinem ecclesie sancte Saltzburgensis*, Venetiis, N. de Franckfordia, 1482; *Breviarium Frisingense*, Pars estivalis, Venetiis, Ioann. Oswalt, 1516; and other German breviaries. In a Cistercian Breviary (Paris, J. Kerver, 1568, 16°) it is the anthem to the canticle at Mattins after the eighth lesson.

The anthem will remind everyone of *Regina caeli laetare.*

This and the following anthems are not noted.

Ave o Theotokos] The first five words of this anthem are in S.B. iii. 140.

Aula Maria] S.B. iii. 136.

INDEX OF PRAYERS, ANTHEMS, RESPONDS, &c.

GENERAL INDEX.

Qui creauit celū lully lully
lu. Nascitur in stabulo byby byby by.
Rex qui regit seculum lully lully lu.
Joseph emit panniculū byby byby by.
Mater inuoluit puerū lully lully lu.
Et ponit in presepio byby byby by.
Inter animalia lully lully lu. Jacet mu

di gaudia byby byby by. Dulcis sup
omnia lully lully lu. Lactat mater dni.
byby byby by. Osculatur puerum lully
lully lu. Et adorat dominu byby byby
by. Roga mater filiu lully lully lu. Ut
det nobis gaudiu byby byby by. In per
enni gloria lully lully lu. In sempitrna

secula byby byby by. In eternu et ultra
lully lully lu. Det nobis sua gaudia.
V. Puer nat est nob.
byby byby by. Concede qs omnipotens deus ut nos
unigeniti tui noua per carne natiuitas
liberet. quos sub peccati iugo uetusta ser
uitus tenet. Per eunde. On shere thurs
day this.
Dominus iesus postqm. ait.
cenauit cum discipulis suis lauit pedes
eorum et ait illis sci tis quid fecerim

The Carol of the Nuns of St. Mary's, Chester (XV. Century)

I have rendered the following Carol into modern notation, from the edition published by the Henry Bradshaw Society in "The Processional of the Nuns of St. Mary's." I have added an alto part, in small notes, so that it may be sung with effect even at the present day.

JOSEPH C. BRIDGE.

Joseph emit panniculum, by, by, etc.
Mater involuit puerum, lully, etc.
Et ponit in presepio, by, by, etc.

Inter animalia, lully, etc.
Jacent mundi gaudia, by, by, etc.
Dulcis super omnia, lully, etc.

Lactat mater domini, by, by, etc.
Osculatur parvulum, lully, etc.
Et adorat dominum, by, by, etc.

Roga mater filium, lully, etc.
Ut det nobis gaudium, by, by, etc.
In perenni gloria, lully, etc.

In sempiterna secula, by, by, etc.
In eternum et ultra, lully, etc.
Det nobis sua gaudia, by, by, etc.

(Reprinted from the Chester Archæological Society's Journal, Vol. XIII.)

HENRY BRADSHAW SOCIETY,

FOR EDITING RARE LITURGICAL TEXTS.

List of Works already issued.

1891. I. MISSALE AD USUM ECCLESIÆ WESTMONASTERIENSIS. fasc. i. Edited by Dr. J. WICKHAM LEGG, F.S.A. 8vo. [Dec. 1891.]

III. THE MARTILOGE, 1526. Edited by the Rev. F. PROCTER, M.A., and the Rev. E. S. DEWICK, M.A., F.S.A. 8vo. [May, 1893.]

1892. II. THE MANNER OF THE CORONATION OF KING CHARLES THE FIRST, 1626. Edited by the Rev. CHR. WORDSWORTH, M.A. 8vo. [Dec. 1892.]

IV. THE BANGOR ANTIPHONARIUM. Edited by the Rev. F. E. WARREN, B.D., F.S.A. Part I. containing complete facsimile in collotype, with historical and palæographical introduction. 4to. [Aug. 1893.]

1893. V. MISSALE AD USUM ECCLESIÆ WESTMONASTERIENSIS, fasc. ii. Edited by Dr. J. WICKHAM LEGG, F.S.A. 8vo. [Aug. 1893.]

VI. OFFICIUM ECCLESIASTICUM ABBATUM SECUNDUM USUM EVESHAMENSIS MONASTERII. Edited by the Rev. H. A. WILSON, M.A. 8vo. [Aug. 1893.]

1894. VII. TRACTS OF CLEMENT MAYDESTONE, viz. DEFENSORIUM DIRECTORII and CREDE MICHI. Edited by the Rev. CHR. WORDSWORTH, M.A. 8vo. [Oct. 1894.]

VIII. THE WINCHESTER TROPER. Edited by the Rev. W. HOWARD FRERE, M.A. 8vo. [Nov. 1894.]

1895. IX. THE MARTYROLOGY OF GORMAN. Edited by WHITLEY STOKES, D.C.L., Foreign Associate of the Institute of France. 8vo. [July, 1895.]

X. THE BANGOR ANTIPHONARIUM, Part II. containing an amended text with liturgical introduction, and an appendix containing an edition of Harleian MS. 7653. Edited by the Rev. F. E. WARREN, B.D., F.S.A. 4to. [Nov. 1895.]

1896. XI. THE MISSAL OF ROBERT OF JUMIÈGES, BISHOP OF LONDON, A.D. 1044–1051, AND ARCHBISHOP OF CANTERBURY IN A.D. 1051. Edited from a MS. in the Public Library at Rouen, by the Rev. H. A. WILSON, M.A. 8vo. [July, 1896.]

XII. MISSALE AD USUM ECCLESIÆ WESTMONASTERIENSIS, fasc. iii. Containing an appendix giving certain Offices from Westminster MSS. in the Bodleian Library and the British Museum, together with full indices, notes, and a liturgical introduction. Edited by Dr. J. WICKHAM LEGG, F.S.A. 8vo. [Nov. 1897.]

1897. XIII. THE IRISH LIBER HYMNORUM. Edited from MSS. in the Libraries of Trinity College, and the Franciscan Convent at Dublin by the Rev. JOHN H. BERNARD, D.D., and ROBERT ATKINSON, LL.D. Vol. I., Text and Glossary.

XIV. Vol. II., Notes and Translations of the Irish Prefaces and Hymns. 8vo. [July, 1898.]

1898. XV. THE ROSSLYN MISSAL. An Irish manuscript in the Advocates' Library, Edinburgh. Edited by the Rev. H. J. LAWLOR, D.D. 8vo. [April, 1899.]

XVI. THE CORONATION BOOK OF CHARLES V. OF FRANCE. Edited by the Rev. E. S. DEWICK, M.A., F.S.A., with reproductions in collotype of the miniatures which illustrate the ceremony. 4to. [In the Press.]

1899. XVII. MISSALE ROMANUM, Milan, 1474. (The first printed edition of the Roman Missal.) Edited by the Rev. ROBERT LIPPE, LL.D. Vol. I. Text. 8vo. [Oct. 1899.]

XVIII. THE PROCESSIONAL OF THE NUNS OF ST. MARY AT CHESTER. With English rubrics. Edited by Dr. J. WICKHAM LEGG, F.S.A. 8vo. [Oct. 1899.]

The following Works are in preparation:

THREE ENGLISH CORONATION ORDERS: (1). The Coronation Order of William III. and Mary II. (2.) An Anglo-French version of the English Coronation Order. (3.) A Pre-Norman Coronation Order. Edited by Dr. J. WICKHAM LEGG, F.S.A. 8vo. [In the Press.]

FACSIMILES OF HORÆ B.M.V., reproduced in collotype from English MSS. of the 11th Century. Edited by the Rev. E. S. DEWICK, M.A., F.S.A. 4to. [In the Press.]

THE HEREFORD BREVIARY. Edited by the Rev. W. HOWARD FRERE, M.A. 8vo. [In the Press.]

ABBOT WARE'S CONSUETUDINARY OF WESTMINSTER. Edited by Sir E. MAUNDE THOMPSON, K.C.B., LL.D., D.C.L., F.S.A. 8vo. [In the Press.]

CLEMENT MAYDESTONE'S DIRECTORIUM SACERDOTUM. Edited by (the late) Rev. Canon COOKE, M.A., and the Rev. CHRISTOPHER WORDSWORTH, M.A.

THE LITURGY OF ST. JAMES. Edited by the Rev. F. E. BRIGHTMAN, M.A.

A MISCELLANEOUS VOLUME CONTAINING:

THE CANON OF THE MASS, AND ITS VARIANTS. Edited by the Rev. H. A. WILSON, M.A., and Dr. J. WICKHAM LEGG, F.S.A.

AN EDITION OF A BODLEIAN MS. (Wood MS. 17) Langforde's *Meditatyons for Goostly Exercyse in the tyme of the Masse.* Edited by Dr. J. WICKHAM LEGG, F.S.A.

A REPRINT OF *Instructio seu Alphabetum Sacerdotum.* Edited by Dr. J. WICKHAM LEGG, F.S.A.

Ordinarium Missæ. From an early 14th Century Sarum Missal formerly in the possession of the late Mr. WILLIAM MORRIS, F.S.A.

A MISCELLANEOUS VOLUME, containing facsimiles of early liturgical MSS., including an early copy of *Quicunque vult*, from an Irish MS. in the Ambrosian Library (O. 212, sup.). 4to.

THE BENEDICTIONAL OF ROBERT OF JUMIÈGES. Edited by the Rev. H. A. WILSON, M.A.

October, 1899.

*** Persons wishing to join the Society are requested to communicate with the Hon. Secretary, the Rev. H. A. WILSON, Magdalen College, Oxford; or with the Hon. Treasurer, the Rev. E. S. DEWICK, 26, Oxford Square, Hyde Park, London, W.

The books are issued to members in return for an annual subscription of one guinea, payable at the beginning of each year.

www.ingramcontent.com/pod-product-compliance
Lightning Source LLC
Chambersburg PA
CBHW020238090426
42735CB00010B/1740
9783337140793